DEaF POETRY NOW!!!

Deaf Poetry Now!!!
An Anthology

Raymond Luczak,
Editor

Handtype Press
Minneapolis, MN

Acknowledgments

The editor wishes to thank Arthur Durkee, Mark Ehrke, Eric Thomas Norris, Tom Steele (*in memoriam*), and Alex Wilhite for their assistance in ways both small and significant with this project. The memories of David Cummer (1956–2022) and André Pellerin (1958–2024) continue to be a blessing.

Jer Loudenback's ASL poem "Deaf Crowds" was translated into English by Raymond Luczak.

Copyright

Handtype Press
PO Box 3941
Minneapolis, MN 55403-0941
Email: handtype@gmail.com
Online: handtype.com

ISBN: 978-1-941960-22-6
Library of Congress Control Number: 2025947547

Printed in the United States of America.

in memoriam

Rex Lowman
(1918–2001)

THE POETS

Poetry Deaf That

One afternoon after work in the summer of 1988, a clean-shaven older man who'd combed his hair to the side and worn a bowtie and a suit jacket strode up across a parking lot to me. I was waiting alone outside Benson Hall for a bus ride to the Union Station off campus. I had graduated from Gallaudet University the month before, but I knew that I would be moving to New York City that September. I was working in Gallaudet's Admissions office and living in a cheap basement apartment while saving up money for the big move.

I was surprised by Rex Lowman's presence; he had never made small talk with me outside class or even right before class. I had studied Economics under him; it was a required elective course. It wasn't the most engaging subject, but his signing was elegant; his fingerspelling precise as the acronyms and numbers and percentages he projected on the screen. It was abundantly clear that he'd taught the course far too many times. I caught flares of his occasional desire to roll his eyes, which he resisted. I had no idea of his age, but if you'd told me back then that he was pushing 70 years, I'd have been shocked. I knew he was older, but he seemed somehow ageless in his bowtie and suit jacket. I knew nothing about his background; only that he was Deaf and had taught Economics for many years at Gallaudet. He never divulged much, if at all, about his upbringing.

When he walked up to me, I was a skinny 22-year-old with strawberry blond hair. Stars were twinkling in my eyes, because I couldn't wait to move to New York. *New York!* I felt the metropolis calling my name, throbbing in my veins. When I saw Manhattan for the first time during my 1985 spring break, I knew that, like the reconteur Quentin Crisp had said about visiting New York for the first time, "I wanted *it*."

When Mr. Lowman strode to my stop, I thought he was there to wait for the campus bus, too. I was quite mistaken. He had something to impart to me, and he wasn't going to make small talk. Oh, no. He simply said in ASL, "There's no future in poetry. It will break your heart."

I was flabbergasted. How did he know that *I* was writing poetry? Who had told him about me? I didn't think I was that good at it. I did love reading and writing poetry, but I wasn't sure if I was worthy of publication. I wasn't even calculating like a professional poet who would submit poems steadily to various journals and magazines in order to rack up a list of credits with an eye toward a book publication. In fact, I wasn't moving to New York to be a writer; I had simply wanted to be in a city far more vibrant than Washington, D.C. Publication was the farthest thing from my mind. Manhattan was a candy store of sensations and experiences, and I wanted to revel in it all.

I don't recall what I'd said to Mr. Lowman, but I most likely asked, "Why are you telling me this?"

"I used to write poetry, but no more."

"You're a poet?"

He nodded.

"I'd love to read your work. Where can I find it?"

"Don't bother."

I glimpsed something I hadn't seen on his face before. If he was occasionally droll with his humor in class, I caught sharp flashes of bitterness. I was immediately intrigued. Did his poetry have such hidden emotions?

"Oh," I said. "I'm sorry if I ..."

"I wish you the best of luck."

"Thank you." I was still in shock. His grasp of the bewildering world of economics had intimidated me. But *him* writing poetry? With my mind blown, I almost missed my bus!

Later, in the campus library, I sought out his work. I rifled through the Dewey index card system (kids, this was *pre*-Internet) for his name, and saw that he had a slender book of poems published in 1964. It was called *Bitterweed*. The concision of his work surprised me. It was fantastic!

I had a difficult time of reconciling my memory of the staid Mr. Lowman with the lines he doled out in his verse. An economist-poet?

Excited, I kept hoping to catch him again on campus, but it was summer. Most of the faculty would not return until August. I didn't know that I'd never see him again.

Mr. Lowman, if you're still flapping your wings somewhere beyond the Pearly Gates, please fly over here. It's my turn to tell you something.

I'm here to tell you that poetry itself has never broken my heart.

Love did.

Death, too.

Maybe you'd equated poetry with love. Or maybe you'd confused poetry with the atrocious "po biz," cliqued beyond belief to elevate their friends and certainly not you or me. I will never know.

Nevertheless, times have changed a great deal in poetry. There are many avenues where a poem can appear. And it's not just the nature of verse itself. The poetry of your youth has been tsunami'd by one movement after another, often blurring genres and expectations. Poetry is not as exclusive as it used to be. A Deaf poet can create a poem in ASL first without expecting it to be translated into English. (Who needs paper, right?) A graphic designer-poet can collage together pictures and text to fashion a "found" poem of sorts. There's sign language gloss poetry, too. (Guilty as charged.) And let's not forget slam poetry! The list is endless.

As long as language exists, poetry will persist even in the cracks of censorship. Language is the biggest power humans have, because with language done right, they can inspire and mobilize change in thought and action.

I only wish you were here now. I don't know how the hell it happened, but I'm now ten years younger than you were the last time I saw you.

I don't know what you'd heard about me in those days, but I still write poetry not because I can but because it's saved me from depression and other ugly things many times over. The power and promise of poetry is this: If I can somehow distill something specific out of my experiences, I have a shot at becoming a photographer for all time. Each poem is a photograph that develops in the darkroom hidden in the reader's head.

I see *you*, Mr. Lowman.

I want you to join me and every reader of this anthology to experience this profusion of emotions by poets regardless of how little or how much they can hear, and regardless of how they prefer to communicate. They all know how to clarify what it means to connect in such messy and embarrassingly human ways.

And it's only just now (!!!) that I've finally grasped why you walked up to me that day. You had most likely felt morally obligated to warn me, but I think you wanted more than that.

You wanted to *connect*. Just like how Deaf people need to nurture each other through the use of Sign, we poets must connect with each other too.

Mr. Lowman, you've been with me all this time.

—Raymond Luczak
Minneapolis, MN

THE POETS

Seen

In the archives of Deaf school museums
In fading little paper family newspapers
I always find you,
The young girl
With black eyes
Who stares back.

You wear monstrous headphones
Or there's a speech teacher
Leaning too close,
Her white hand
Touching your throat.

Your eyes speak to me.
They tell of equal parts
Desperation, near resignation.

Deaf eyes to Deaf eyes,
I want to tell you
I see you.

I want to tell you
I see too
Unawakened joy.

It's there,
Resting in the lap
Of your perfectly pressed
Skirt—
A small,
Clenched fist.

Karen Christie

Initiation

Lyla doesn't remember much
Of her childhood
Before she learned sign language.
But she remembers clearly
That first sign.

It was also her first time
At the Deaf school
Where she walked beside her mother—
Wearing her shiny black shoes—
Down the shiny-floored hallway.

She looked over her shoulder,
As a group of kids were rushed
Into their classroom.
The last, a boy,
Waved wildly at her
And then she noticed
His other sleeve was empty.

As the classroom door closed,
Her mother guided her further on
Into the room with high desks
And frowning adults.

Later, a girl about her age
Came in
Swinging her braids
Eying Lyla up and down
Shyly smiling.

The girl led her out
And back down the hall they went.
Braid girl's hands going up and down and all around.

Lyla felt she should understand
This nodding Braid girl.

At the very end of the hall, Braid girl pointed to a door.
Her face took on a wide-eyed horror—
Shaking her head and her finger.
And then,
Her right index finger
Chopped down
Near her left elbow.

Later, Lyla would learn
This was the sign PUNISH.
But at that moment
Lyla wondered
How many more
Empty sleeves
There were
In the school.

Karen Christie

To Those Old Deaf Men

When the door to the Deaf club was opened for me,
They must have seen it from the start
Spying me across the gaming tables and folding chairs.

Their eyes would widen and at some point
I'd be waved over to where
They always sat
To where
Their bodies had carved
Their forms into the chairs
As they watched
Comings and goings.

And before I even sat down,
One would start to tell a joke.
Maybe the one about the Deaf honeymooners
Or the Deaf worker fooling his Hearing boss,
Carefully checking
With his bright eyes
Just to see
If I understood enough …

When the joke ended,
I'd laugh along uncertainly.
All around the table folks would swat arms—
FUNNY NOTHING, someone would say.
SAME OLD, NOTHING NEW, someone else would sigh.
They'd chuckle still.

Then, another would share an anecdote,
KNOW HAPPEN WHAT.
I would noddingly follow along
A signed path describing the ghost of a Deaf child's face.
He would pause and check, UNDERSTAND?

A face that could often be seen at his old Deaf school
Gazing out at night from the second-floor dorm
With almost-understanding, I'd awkwardly sign, WOW, TRUE???
Many have seen it, he would swear.

And then, I'd see the wink there.
They would all laugh and point at me.
THIS-ONE, they'd tell others,
BIG FISH SWALLOW.
A woman nearby would dismiss it all, saying to me, WARN-YOU,
    BELIEVE HIM NOTHING.

The old men would tease further—
Using fake name signs, exaggerated gossip
Mixed in with some wild true club history,
All the while side-eyeing me …
Teaching me
The fine art of catching
That hint of a teasing-eye glimmer.

Ah, those old Deaf men
Over the years, I saw them sitting in clubs in Oakland, Portland,
    Pittsburgh, and Rochester,
Playing cards, telling stories,
Always watching the door.

PEACE and WAR

The sign PEACE
In American Sign Language
Is not the same as
The two-fingered gesture folks use.

The sign PEACE
In American Sign Language
Is far more complicated than that.

For this sign,
Cupped hands at opposite sides of the body
Close the space between them—
Until they meet as partners
And lightly embrace
Like the sign MARRIAGE.

These gently joined hands then
Move like the sign FRIEND.
But the signs, FRIEND and MARRIAGE,
Consists of only two
Whereas the sign PEACE
Requires many.

The lightly clasped hands
Of this community of friends
Then calmly separate,
Spreading fingers
Flow outward
Reaching to touch us all
Like the sign
BLESSING.

*

The sign WAR
In American Sign Language
Is simpler than the sign
For PEACE.

The hands of the sign WAR communicate
Communities divided
Like soldiers lined up, facing each other
Across an abyss.

Ready to fire,
These squads tensely retreat and advance
Back and forth
Like the sign for STRUGGLE.

Back and forth, back and forth
The sign WAR
Can be dragged out
As armed conflicts are.

Many other signs
That require the full commitment
Of two hands—
COMMUNICATION,
NEGOTIATION,
TRUST,
HOPE—
Are needed
To recover
The blessing
Of peace.

charlie ainsworth

Words

Your mouth moved—
Words floated toward me.
I reached out,
but they stopped mid-air.

You saw me,
then saw my silence.
"Never mind," your face said.
"Not worth the effort."

What was it?
A thought, a feeling, a question?
A secret that I should not hear?
Or just a passing nothing?

You carried it away,
as if I couldn't hold it.
As if my hands were too small
to catch your meaning.

I watched it leave,
watched you leave.
You took the bridge with you
and left me on this side, alone.

Not worth the effort,
not worth the words.

Slow . . . Crash

His speech too rapid
His speech then slow
Slow I get it
Slow I repeat it
It being what he said
It being what I think he said
Said urgently
Said repeatedly
Repeatedly not rephrasing
Repeatedly not understanding
Understanding the command
Understanding so demanding
Demanding my comprehension
Demanding my undivided attention
Attention to the words
Attention to the details
Details I try to grasp
Details beyond my grasp
Grasp the meaning
Grasp the warning
Warning about a bike
Warning sounds that sound alike
Brkl
  mph
    kids
Brkl
  no
    ykl
      fizz

Crash . . .

They   shine   pitiful sm   iles

Intolerable this evening
My husband and I clean and weed the garden
set the table with silk placemats
I heat rolls of filo dough filled with cheese
Our guests pile in
happy to escape the unbearable outdoor heat
I hand each of them a glass of lemonade
Thank you for having us
Of course, of course
So-and-so please meet so-and-so
So nice to meet you

Lips   run   a mile   a minute

Straining to catch bits of banter
I gawk at my phone's captioning app which displays
"Okay"
"Okay"
"Yeah"
"Okay"
"And"

I ask one guest, an old friend,
Learn sign language (I sign *hello*)
I can't (He *waves hand*)
Yes, you can (*hello*)
No, no (*waves hand flatly*)
Feels like a slap
I squint
He turns away

How was I, I later ask my husband
Great, he says, exuberant
Great, I say, deflated

Deaf and Waiting to Join the Conversation

Have you ever been told
HOLD—

This poem is on hold.

Middle Finger

Allow
me to
get this
off my
chest. I
don't feel
confident
socially,
language
is a pain
in the ass,
and I hate
feeling judged by those who think
they know the vernacular better than I do.
Not saying I'm perfect, just saying
I'm sick and tired of being judged
by those who think they are.

Black High-Heeled Shoes

My husband was away at one of his multitudinous
business meetings—conferences and seminars and department
motivational retreats, I can't remember which—
for me, they were a string of beads I no longer threaded
but dropped with disregard,
spilling uncontrollably across the floor,
rolling freely under the bosom of our kitchen table
where we ate our breakfasts, past the comfy chairs
where we would recline and read the newspaper
and continue far beneath the nearby sofa
in the family room where we would sit together
when he was home and watch a captioned show.

I declined invitations to attend his conferences
where I would find myself adjusting my hearing aid
over and over again to capture some sense of sound
and the exact issue being discussed, or joke shared,
or question asked, without having to pause
and ask the bearer of good or bad or funny tidings
to repeat him or herself—which they did—
each retelling similar to echoes in a cave,
carbon copies increasingly blurry, diffuse,
deflated repetitions with each retelling.

I remember, once, my husband invited me to fly to whatever city
he was inhabiting at the moment for some celebratory dinner.
I can't remember the reason for the urgency of my presence,
but I do remember I wanted to make sure I was still
his primary motivation in his life, his *raison d'etre*,
his will to succeed, his soul's reckoning.
So, I went and purchased a black dress with an open back
and thin spaghetti straps with a length that followed my curves
to just below my knees and, of course,
I had to buy a pair of black shoes to match

and went to a high-end store.
A nice middle-aged gentleman helped me in my quest
to buy the sexiest high-heeled shoes I could find,
his bald head reflecting the recessed light above us
like a misguided spotlight.
He brought me all kinds of fancy black shoes—
open-toed, closed-toed, pumps, sandals with skinny heels—
I tried them all on, wasn't sure of any of them
until he slid the sole of my foot
into a stylish yet comfortable cradle
with a solid yet slim heel, a strap of fine leather
stretched across the instep
touching the cleavage of my toes.
What sold me on this particular shoe, though,
were the beads of sweat materializing
on the smoothness of the top of the shoe salesman's head
as he set my foot like Cinderella,
yes, this is the shoe, and this is the foot to fill it,
and I purchased it.

The shoes I did not keep,
as painful bunions and cartilage tears
prevent me from wearing such a shoe these days,
but oh, the delightful memory
of purchasing them, of wearing them,
the glow on my husband's face when he saw me,
a pyre of desire released,
his chase after me across the dance floor
like two sparrows racing across the sky.

Payphone

you are a receiver, a deliverer of sound,
is mine lost in transit?

you swallow my coin
you taunt me, 20 seconds of

timed silence, the screen says zero,
you gave me that at twenty

Hello? Can you hear me? I can't hear you, speak louder

you can see me thumping my
heart, I'm showing you,

you don't turn up,
you trap me in a box

you make me feel stranded
even the vibrations at the

back of my dry inflamed
throat can't shatter

your windows, I look out of them, praying,

you turn my contacts into numbers,
defunct buttons on a keypad,

you offer captions on the glass,
in graffiti, red, oversized words,

yesterday's conversations that show
the caller wants to go to hell

michael isaacs

please tell me, find a way, surely you
owe me that much?

you spit out my last coin
onto the cold metal.

you end the call,
did it ever begin?

Adapt for Us

Adapt for us
Let sounds drift through the vibrations of the floor,
Don't leave us waiting behind your otherworldly door.

Adapt for us
Read my lips and let me read yours,
Manage this and we'll wave our hands with a silent applause.

Adapt for us,
Make our language part of every school's curriculum scheme,
Sign language accessible for all, the deaf community's dream.

Adapt for us,
Here's a notepad and pen,
please kindly use it and note down for us; what, where, who and when.

Adapt for us
Put words on all screens,
let accurate subtitles guide us, through every important scene.

Adapt for us
Have a loop system in place,
and remember to always reserve us a front row space.

Adapt for us
We are the deaf community.

michael isaacs

The Trailblazers

Here's to the trailblazers,
searching like stargazers,
for alternatives to sound,
fabled frequencies finally found,
sounds new mediums, new guises,
translating noise sends super suprises,
sound dressed in serene shapes
hands dancing, noise won't escape,
sound wearing words and notes,
sound wearing different coats,
sound reading words on lips
sound leaping off a tongue's tip,
sound vibrating through fingertips,
sound waves felt when the music whips,
sound of speech printed on captions,
sound captions capturing reactions,
sound of voices with no problem repeating,
sounds of kindness whose hearts are beating.

I Am

I've never been taught by rabbis
who'd teach me to be a Jew
or schooled in places where
they'd teach me to know what I am.

I've been manipulated by psychologists,
speech therapists, special needs teachers,
audiologists, and who knows who else,
to epitomize selflessness,
and transcend the hearing aid—
they never taught me to know who I am.

I've among merchants who'd
thought a pledged membership
to the synagogue wouldn't
make them rich—but never took them
time to teach me to know what I am.

I've worked with many colleagues
whose detached identity was more
important than themselves. Glory
was served by the basketful—
it didn't show me who I am.

I've had to find myself
in a boxful of puzzle pieces.
Nothing was missing! They all fitted
into a picture—
a cracked mirror.

Cobweb in the Corner

A quiet spot in a noisy room—
hardly a breeze would whiff to nudge
a cobweb in the corner,

a little spider sitting atop
waiting for a tired bug
to loiter about
the cobweb in the corner.

A fly flies by to perch
only to know—without a chance—
there's no way to let go
the cobweb in the corner.

A deaf guy sat in the noisy room,
hardly a hearing person noticed.

A lonely hearing guy
sat coyly a few chairs away,
noticing the other guy
at the other end of the wall,

stood up and went by
to pay a chat
only to learn—much to his chagrin—
he couldn't say anything with his hands.

Deaf Pariah

I'm a distant man
A social animal
Alone in the crowd
I only listen and watch.
I laugh
I cry—
I won't let it show.

My deep thoughts.
My strange dreams.
Some I share
but no one needs to know.

Whether I sign
or talk—

I just conform when I need to.

My conflagrant soul smiles—
Where else can I go?

Beyond the Deaf Mountain

> The phantom
> horn writes in its loss,
> walls its ancient lament
> beyond the deaf mountain.
> —"Ram's Horn" by P. Garfinkel

Someone mentioned
hearing echoes
between the peaks
distant sounds
echoing grotesquely
among snowcapped crags
among mangling jags.

I feel as if I'm climbing
toward the pointed sheer sky
if only the ear horn would say
where He'd be found.

Mountain
foliating solidarity
where detouring winds
pass winding paths
carving chipped nicks
footing scree steps—
choreographing
the alpine sweep.

The climb
the scramble
the reach
the pointed sheer sky

someone mentioned
hearing the ear horn blowing—
I didn't quite catch it.

Evening Hike

Hiking in the forest
not far from the house,
an evening of taupe sky.

Gliding hawk-like birds
have long left for the day.
Fleeting jays haven't stopped by yet.

Sparrows
titmice
cardinals
chickadees
robins
and finches
and squirrels
still scurried by occasionally
when countered.

The serene creek
mulling through
decomposing mulch
hopping over fallen trees among
decaying leaves,
skunk cabbage
daunted by nibbling cottontails.

A bridging log scampered
the creek rolling under.

Swarming, pestering, minute gnats.

It's time I left
or I'll lose
the patronizing full moon.

In the Melting In Between
East Osceola, 4156'

My whole life, my deafness
follows me like an imaginary friend,
signing in my head, a gift
or a boon, I don't always
get to choose which, every
mouth, set of hands, body I must translate
is another mountain to climb.

Some summits are invisible,
viewless except for their trees
and a small cairn.

My gender is invisible, too.

Every time I reach one of these summits,
I revel in the search for it, sometimes
the cairn is covered by snow, and I feel the same
kinship, familiar sensation—
neither here nor there—is this the top?

I look like one thing, but feel like
another. No one who sees me once
would know—this secret I hold,
I choose my makeup every day but
my inner faces make their own choices,
moss grows in my crevices, laced
with ice as it is in spring and again in fall, changing
seasons mirror the shifting inside me,

like this trail through mossy trees, where the usnea
hangs low, I feel at one with the unexpected
patches of icy snow that hide—a shock of white within the green—
winter delaying its departure for as long as it can,

the ice will eventually melt into pools of water,

I am most comfortable there
in the melting in between,

from the rubbery feet of the mushrooms
to the feathery edges of the moss—both so much a part
of the trees you cannot tell where one ends
and the other begins—

Aren't they all connected, in tune, sweeping
parts of a whole world, a mountain
that cares little for deafness or
gender, a trail that passes a summit and
unceremoniously continues
down the other side?

Ice that Cuts
North Twin, 4761'

There are places in this world
where the cliff faces are things
we read like runes, name as if
in a name, we can gift them a life.

But these mountains know more
than we do. They've risen from earth-
shattering dreams, moved so slowly
we couldn't see it. Instead, we climb,

packs full of gadgets to measure height of land,
wind speeds, temperatures. How cold
before I need my gloves, or this hat
I've tucked away, this neck warmer I've hidden?

We climb, each step we feel the weight
of every emergency item we've carried,
yet people are still freezing to death up here,
still bringing hardly anything or too much

weight that kills, gear that saves. The difference
between life and death gets closer the colder
it is, yet we cannot stop ourselves from racing
up to the edge of that line, threading our life

through the branches of the spruces trapping
you in their secret holes, the ice that cuts like
knives against bare calves in springtime. Every
step out here is a journey I long for—

this wild world, meeting trees in the places
where they sing, meeting cliff faces

where they rise at such an angle, you need
to grip the trees to climb—I hike

to put my life in the boughs of a birch tree,
I know it's strong enough before I let go,
I lean my head against its wrapped skin.
In this moment, I am more alive than yesterday.

The Kind We Tell Legends About
Madison, 5367'

A mountain is as personal
as the cuts it gives me when I
crash to my knees from the effort
of the climb, not in prayer,

but it's the same as prayer—we suffer
up the rough terrain, past the same wide
trees with gaping mouths and eyes,
birds nesting in their hollows.

A mountain that brings us down on
our knees is the kind we tell legends
about. The one we return to again
and again, if only, to test our resolve,

see how many times we can fall,
and avoid falling. It moves us without
being moved in return. We climb and
we learn the secrets of its stoicism,

in the ways only the trees arch and change
with the years that pass, the snow, wind,
and rain that brings them to the ground,
turns their bark into mushrooms and bryophytes.

Deliberations of an Ending

I am watching my tiny screen, thumb
on fire, cramping with constant motion,
as the world explodes
a little more each hour, passing from
one dark to another, indigo to burgundy—

can I claw my eyes out yet?

I'm not sure how I wanted this to end—
I promise I had more hope at some
point in time moving faster until we can't
listen anymore, the words jumble

the more they warp, bent backwards from
pressure, the tight squeeze
of a rich man's hand around
the world, as if it were the soft neck
of a human they used to fuck

it's the easy way they use words,
how they roll off tongues, send
viruses through the wires, fingers
turn to shock waves, spreading under

skin, already inside, writing with our own blood—

Red Ribbon

Losing the myopic view
of long gone events.
Allowing them to fade
into the fog of history.
Regaining perspective
and proportion. Birth
announcement. Flattened
booties. First drawing
of the kitty. Photo of her
holding Maxie when he
was just a puppy. Macaroni
necklace. Recital award.
The poem about a dinosaur.
Doily Valentine: "To Mom.
Love, Rosie." Dale's letter,
"Come to Alaska with me."
Threw everything with the
funeral notice, the memoir
transcript, even the red ribbon,
into a box in the basement.

2025

martha ellen

Terminal Diagnosis

Sis called. 11:00 pm.
She needed a pen.
[She didn't know.]
I dream of a cougar
sleeping next to me.
Don't move a muscle.
Slowly I cover my
jugular with my hand.
The least I could do.

2012–2024

Bits and Pieces of Danger

I could write down every single
time I was in extreme danger—
the gun pointed at me, the assaults
I escaped, the failed plot to murder me,
the threats of rape, the menacing,
the fast talk to get away—and toss
them up into the air and let them
land like scraps on the sewing room
floor or bits and pieces of junk discarded
along some back road. I could pick
them up as they lay, bind them
together for some prize-winning
quilt or marvelous sculpture.

2025

Plied Worlds

Sometimes I can feel the layering
of time, different worlds plied, past
over present. The day I needed to buy
some red ribbon, bombs exploded
on Commercial Street.
"Hello. Enjoying the sunshine?"
The Beast knocked in Bruges.
"*Öffne die Tür!*"
"Yes, a little too hot for me."

Then, in *sotto voce*, "They took my
four uncles into the woods. Never seen again."
I told her, "My Tante went missing, too."
Amid the distant gunshots we heard them calling.
"*Denk aan ons.*" Remember us.

But not today. All's quiet. She hands me
a receipt. We smile like strangers. I leave
and head for home. There is only a light
breeze on this warm and sunny day.

2024

Aeschylus and My Brother

Yesterday I received a call from my brother.
My sister-in-law perished. Leukemia. Her
death was swift and unexpected. He had
her body cremated and spread her ashes
by the pond on their farm. She loved the pond,
especially at sunset. They walked there often.

"I couldn't control my feelings for two days,"
he apologized. [I understood. In our family
no one shed tears. Emotions were not permitted.
That piece of the human puzzle was torn to bits,
burnt to ashes and tossed out with the trash.]

"Even in our sleep the pain that cannot
forget falls drop by drop upon the heart,
and in our own despair, against our will,
comes wisdom to us by the awful
grace of God." [Drifting through my
mind, woven through his words.]

He said he researched "leukemia" for
cerebral, objective documentation. Had
a better understanding of her death. He
whispered to me, "I heard her voice call
my name." He dreams now. Lying by
the pond at sunset, her ashes dry his tears.

2024

martha ellen

Progress in Therapy

All of my life I've had
"telephone nightmares."
The telephones change, though.
[Jung and Freud would love this.]
It's always the same theme:
I'm in grave danger. I must "call"
for help. The phone never,
ever works. I wake up.

Last night another one.
I found the "smart" phone
down the block tied to a gate.
Try as I may, it never connected
with whoever could rescue me.

But last night, after the danger
had passed, the phone worked!!!!!
The police dispatch answered.
"Martha, help is on the way."
I looked out the window and
saw them arrive with all the gear
they needed to investigate
and solve the case. They knocked.
I could not unlock the door.

Progress.

2025

O Mother Moon

in memory of Vera, my mother, on her birthday (August 4, 2017)

[*The poem alternates between English and ASL gloss.*]

O mother moon in the sky—

> Palm-at-moon mother (old sign using two hands nearly
> grandmother) dark moon (C not bend "L") sky (2 palms)

Thou are the most illuminating beauty of all in the night.

> Still-hold-moon and using left hand) A-L-L sky thou wow
> shine beautiful

Mother moon's moonbeams beaming on our faces remind us
of her caresses of love and inspiration with her constant feeding,
support, encouragement, and love so we could grow into better people.

> All palms people look-up mother moon moonbeams shine on-
> face like mother (role shifting) hand-caressing-face
> inspire mother feed-feed encourage-encourage support-support
> love give grow-grow become what good person (BB hands)

O mother moon, thy smile—oh how we miss you greatly.
Nonethless, we are happy when we see the mother moon
come and go in the everlasting cycles, we will always
remember you without "memory go away."

> Thou mother dark moon disk smile
> Wow (hold bend "C" from smile sign) we really-really miss you
> me touch-heart (sigh) but (both palms) we happy see what?
> (hold open finger hands) mother moon land moon—up moon—
> down cycle look-up forget never.

The Leaf

an ASL poem using two "five" handshapes

5   tree-sign
55 big-trunk-up to top
55 spread-branches
55 leaf-at-end-of branch
5   leaf-lightly-motion
55 raining
55 leaf-at-end-of branch-hit-by-rain-and-tremble
55 strong-gust-of-wind
55 leaf-at-end-of branch-sway-break out
5   gliding-across-mid-section
5   gliding-across-lower
55 ground-leaf-landing
55 ground-snowing-across-mid-section
55 ground-snowing-across-lower
55 ground-snow-cover-leaf

The Bug
an ASL numbers poem

[in ASL gloss]

1   point
2   me-see
3   bug
4   crawl
5   hands up and scream!
6   bug, scared, jump!
7   antennae flicker
8   me-hate-it!
9   me-not-like
10 me-squish-thumb and rub-shirt clean-off-thumb

[in English]

As I strolled and checked around,
I suddenly saw something!
A bug
As it crawled across!
It made me scared.
The bug, also scared, jumped away,
With its antennae shivering!
How I hate bugs
And really despise them!
So I squished the bug with my thumb,
And rub on my shirt to clean off.

O Mighty Columbia River!

[Mime: Mother carries baby while rocking as she signs.]

See that river
O Mighty Columbia River!
Its wide river that rolling on,
Rolling on and on
No matter how high or low,
Still flowing on
Whenever you are happy or low,
Look for the river
Still flowing on and on,
That water is your life.

When I grow up until ten years old
Me moving to a strange school in strange town of Vancouver
My parents left without an explanation
Lucky me, the school on top of the hill
Looking over the Columbia River!

O Mighty Columbia River!
Its wide river that rolling on,
Rolling on and on
No matter how high or low,
Still flowing on
Whenever I am happy or low,
Look for the river
Still flowing on and on,
That water is my life.

Then all the years I worked
Travel nearly the entire United States
There's no home like Washington State!
When I moved back and whenever I saw Columbia River
My heart smiles

O Mighty Columbia River!
Its wide river that rolling on,
Rolling on and on
No matter how high or low,
Still flowing on
Whenever I am happy or low,
Look for the river
Still flowing on and on,
That water is my life.

Then I met someone
I moved away to start the family
Leaving my sweet state behind
Have been away for 15 years
What luck I got the job at Central Washington University at
    Ellensburg, Washington!
One day I got the chance to drive to say hello to the Columbia River ...

O Mighty Columbia River!
Its wide river that rolling on,
Rolling on and on
No matter how high or low,
Still flowing on
Whenever I am happy or low,
Look for the river
Still flowing on and on,
That water is my life.

Now I am home.

Deaf Crowds

I went to a huge—I mean, *huge*—Deaf event.
I didn't want to go, but a friend twisted my arm,
begging me to come along for company.

I finally relented despite knowing that
over 14,000 people would be attending.

So: I went. I'm the type of person who prefers
logistical stuff, as in making sure everything flowed
together for the attendees. *That?* No. No.

My body felt as if it was petrified!

It was the visual equivalent of how hearing people
hated the sound of fingernails scratching a blackboard.
My eyes felt that when I saw the crowds.

Even worse were the vendors area with their nice booths.
The aisles were quite narrow where Deaf people clogged
the pathway. It was difficult to navigate
around them talking close together.
I had to say, "Excusemeexcusemeexcuseme."

At times it wasn't even safe to walk past them!
Their flat hands while signing would fly past me,
almost slapping my face, my forehead, my ears.

Sometimes their pointed fingers looked ready to jab me,
and I had to duck. *Do I want to go
through that again?* N. O.

A Sestina for the Deaf

In the early hours of the morning,
a Goldfinch in a maple tree by the window
lip-syncs a voiceless melody.
Far above, a helicopter hovers in the sky
without the sputtering of an engine,
and the water roaring from a garden hose is silent.

While you behold the silent
wheels of a passing truck this morning
without the roaring of an engine,
a howling dog presses its nose on the window
to sniff the coming of rain from the sky
after hearing the thunder belt a peaceful melody.

You did not waltz to the melody
of the sputtering engine that is silent,
or the gentle grumbling in the sky,
nor did you sway this morning
to the laughter that slithered through a window,
so loud as the placid engine.

What matters is that the engine
of your heart sings a poignant melody,
and the music from the window
of your soul is the silent
moving of hands in the morning
amidst the fury of clouds gathering in the sky.

Even though there's a silent sky,
Even though there's a silent engine
in a silent morning,
Even though there's a silent melody
in a stillness that's silent,
there's a jovial window

in your soul. A window
where the sky
is never silent,
where the engine
is a peaceful melody
in the morning.

Let your hands draw an engine!
Let your hands paint a sky!
Let your hands sketch a morning!

Black Deaf Woman

I'm a Black Deaf woman
I'm the one Lucille Clifton wrote a poem about
talking about these hips that sure don't fit in "small spaces"

I'm a Black Deaf woman
Oh! I'm pure-pure pure jazz!
If Billie Holiday were here, she'd say, "You go, Black Deaf Woman!"

Yes, I'm a Black Deaf woman
My Black Deaf dopeness, e be plenty, e be so *boku* in Lagos, Nigeria;
in Brixton, London, and even in Harlem

I'm a Black Deaf woman
So *una* wan tell me
that my deafness be asymptote to dumbness?
Imma serve you a sweet dose of poetic resistance
As a matter of fact, I got a pocketful of poems for you!

I'm a Black Deaf woman
Hey you, scoot over!
I wanna front-row seat with Aja Monet and Khadijah Queen

I'm a Black Deaf woman
Tonight, imma be Maya Angelou
Imma recite poems that spiral sky-high to the Sixth Stanza of the G

I'm a Black Deaf woman
Yes!
I'm a Black Deaf woman!

Juxtaposition

A little brown boy
dashes to the corner store
and returns
with bullet holes
and the dreaded stench
of death.

A little white boy
strolls to the town bakery
and returns
with cinnamon buns
and the glorious scent
of molasses.

On Brooklyn Bridge

Giant metallic rhapsodies
bloom on a mile-long walk
across the Brooklyn Bridge
one September afternoon.

The passing engines screech
melodies that are *mort* to me—
it is the cadence of faces
that caress my tympanums.

Halfway by a guarding lamp
I pause to stare
at the choral hues of *liberte*—
bright-yellow shadows of lovers entwined
blue octaves of silent prattle
the red settling crescendo of the sun
green baritones of moving clouds
and the orange tempo of a hopping dove.

It is here that we hear
the bliss of dreams that now breathe.

It is here that we hear
the swaying of bodies in unity.

Ghosted

You didn't even give me a chance
to bring out the china and
brew a pot of tea while soliciting which
back-breaking Kama Sutra position you desire.

You didn't even give me a chance
to lick the tiny drops of
sweat masquerading
behind the fuzzy hairs of
your withered manhood.

You didn't even give me a chance
to listen to lies of why your
shirt has the scent of your
long-dead aunt.

You didn't even give me a chance
to try on a plethora of white gowns
and run mad for a day,
all in the name of discarding my last name.

You didn't even give me a chance
to dreamily tell a sistah friend that
"oh, he's really a combo of a
rainy-day-got-nothing-to-do-jazz
and coconut juice."

Ode to January

You are the firstborn of twelve,
wiping away glitzy desires wrapped
in haste before the twenty-fifth of the last,
and after the last's hasty departure,
you come bearing wishes of regrets never resurrecting.

Perhaps you feel a tinge of jealousy
for the sixth and seventh with
their fiery days of scantily dressed teenagers,
possessed soloists on metallic stages,
and violent bursts of psychedelic panorama.
Do not fret over your eleven siblings,
for you are the wittiest of them all,
with your promises of a svelte body and proper habits.

You are the warmth of fireplaces.
A whispering kettle on the stove.
A chimney birthing smoke.
Icicles peering through the window
at lovers conjoined under a protruding blanket.

Janvier is what Paris calls you
in the midst of a snow-covered Seine.
You are unpredictably *Ichigastsu* in Japanese.
Your dichotomy is the envy of a single-minded man.
At the snap of a breeze,
you disrobe your frigid stillness
and march as *Januari* to Mombasa
to watch camels trample warm sand
by ink-blue waters.

If we do not die during your reign,
there will be plenty of time for us
to gather the stormy dreams of tomorrow.

Lake Michigan

Ocean overflowed the edges of my mind.
Unlike the lakes of home, I couldn't see across Lake Michigan,
and so, I believed it must really be an ocean.
But then I swam in the real ocean and learned
that its waves were alive and its body tasted of tears.
When my head emerged from grey-green water, I licked salt from
     my lips. I stood where the waves crested and crashed into foam,
     watching each wave curl toward me,
slap cold and hard against my shins, then dwindle into a moving white
     web
over brown sand. Deeper, where the water reached my shoulders, it
     lifted me gently
and set me down again, never in quite the same place. My head was
     a small, unanchored buoy, marking the spot where my body
     dangled below.

Lilacs

In the corner of the room sit two small canvases you painted
for me. They are little boxes of color, one with flowers
spilling over its sides. Lilacs! I thought, when I unwrapped it.
No, cherry blossoms, you said.
You would visit, you said, but then
you couldn't come. Somewhere among cross-stacked piles
of white paper covered in poems, a chain of handwoven stars
is buried. Another gift from you, those stars are waiting for me
to dance them into open air.
Sometimes I get the urge to decorate, but the colorful things remind me
of you. The walls are still white.

Fireflies

Barefoot on the lawn,
toes curling into the grass
we tried not to blink
as we scanned the night air.

We darted to each tiny eye
that winked open,
glowing vivid green,
then closed to black lash-wings
we strained to see.

We sensed our moments,
leapt, and closed empty hands,
until, triumph!
We peered
into the space
of a prayer, in thrall,
to each illumination
of cathedrals between our palms.

Though Many People Are Amazed or Afraid, Deaf Scholars and Community Members React with Excitement to the Recent Discovery That Spiders Communicate Using Sign Language

following a silk strand from Thomas Lux

A few of the more unorthodox American Sign Language comparative linguists fashion suction cups the size of tarantula knees and others to fit the interphalangeal joints of the human hand. They begin to record data on the precise angles of each position of each joint.

The comparative linguists spend hours at a time observing spider movements. They must control their urges to search for morphemes at this early juncture. They often forget to eat.

At night, when they are not quite asleep, the comparative linguists' legs and arms twitch them into sudden alertness, afterimages of waving hairy limbs fading from the screens of their sleeping minds.

Deaf neurolinguists question ratios of brain size to vocabulary size. While learning to read jumping spider brain waves, they adjust to using tiny tools with minimal exploding of spider heads.

The neurolinguists wonder, given the enormity of species diversity in terms of both spider body size and geographic habitat, whether this work will continue for the rest of their careers.

Deaf ethicists debate the value of measuring the spider sign language against our own, whether we could possibly overcome bias in doing so, and whether it is more ethical to name the local language "SSL" or "ASL (arachnid variation)" or leave it unnamed until we understand what the spiders call it, themselves?

Deaf philosophers ask whether we can know that spiders are not studying us.

Museums and zoos with live spider collections are keen to have Deaf staff on site.

Parents encourage their children to go into the field of Arachnology.

Deaf children mob the spider exhibits after school. The younger children watch keenly through the glass, mimicking taps and waves. They furtively discuss how to set the spiders free, and the older children snicker.

messenger goose

summer sunlight springs through
rows of double paned windows
set in whitewashed cement blocks
a coat of old school floor wax
glows on the cold linoleum tiles
checkerboarded in purple and white

above
a solitary fly
outcast by swatting palms
seeks solace from its exile
in a fluorescent bulb's flickering buzz
and watches with dizzied abandon

below
a troop of girls
in decorated green sashes sit
duck duck goose-style
in the stale school cafeteria
walled in by soup-stained tables

small hands cupped over ears
shoulders hunched against
breathy whispers itching ear canals
snickering eyes squeezed shut
each leans over to brace the next girl's ear
tickles her with feathery fricatives

i pretend
the tinny hisses whistles clicks
the geysers of hot air
blasted directly into my hearing aid
don't hurt

s. leigh ann cowan

i wince
hunch my shoulders
then remember to giggle
i am just like them

i wiggle a finger against the ear mold
massage away the ringing
with pickled static as
i invent a sentence to whisper
it's out of my hands

that's not what I said at all
the amazed cadet laughs
squinting eyes seeking
the goose among ducks

they stop
upon me
the air thrums
as the thunderous A/C spurs on
gooseflesh prickles across my arms

i cast my eyeline to the cadet
and await her judgement
the verdict gurgles along
vintage tin cans and looped string
underwater
my feet paddle frantically

i try to hide the telltale feathers
an egg forms in my throat
it breaks sharp and i taste
bitter yolk and ignominy

the cadet stands imposing
fists akimbo brows nosediving
she calls me out

of the friendship circle

can you at least try a little?
you're ruining the game
for the other girls

it's not fair

i lift the tin can phone
please leave
a message
after the bean

then i turn tail and run
cans clattering behind
the wind pushes and gushes
against my weighted ears
fomenting an ocean
to drown out the noise

i cast line after line for
plentiful iridescent fish
but they are already caught
writhing in the bills of ducks
we share a bland gape
as i cast about once more

the tin can string pulls taut
sings like a live piano wire
fish hooked by crooked finger
to the other end at last

i place the receiver over my ear
overfilled with unaiding aid
and hear a cacophony of
non[s]en[s]

s. leigh ann cowan

i say
say again

non[s]EN[s]

i echo
say again

NON[s]EN[s]

i honk
say again

Never mind.

a goose's noose!
i flee the lasso
in spiraling figure eights
frayed feathers flying
webbed feet slapping and slipping

into the can i speak
as best i can
with a clumsy beak
please don't pluck the messenger
just give me more time
one more chance
honk
i mean quack

i break for the friendship circle
elbowing my way in
displacing others to take my place
sitting as prim and pretty
as the rest of the ducks on display

the cadet tastes alphabet soup

tying noodles in knots
with an expert tongue
encrypting a new message
to nourish the troop

i take the moment to remove
my hearing aids and drop them
into the tin can—plunk clunk—
cover it with a palm and give it a shake
i roll them, hoping for luck
and residual fish sauce to relish

the aids come out
tarred and feathered
batteries buzzing
my hopes fly
i swat them away

the message creeps
word by word
slipping from slithering tongues
of giggling girls
each shimmers iridescent green
aglow with infinite knowledge and amity

as the girl beside me turns
licking her bill
i press the canned aids into my ears
slick with preservatives
and await
my daily bowl of secret word soup

i cringe
and hunch my shoulders
against the static
blast of air
i hear …

s. leigh ann cowan

i hear ... !
the incomprehensible certainty of
non[s]en[s]

the ducks watch me
quack says one duck
quack coughs another
i place a can to my ear
the other to my beak

i say
honk

i hear
non[s]en[s]

i lean to the girl beside me
sitting criss cross applesauce
enfold my wings around her ear
and hiss ...
i'll tell you later.

Dinner Table Syndrome

I'm finally free ...
No longer a family dog ...
No more anxiety ...
No more feeling sadness ...
No more broken promises from family members saying they will
    include me at the dinner table ...
No more getting frustrated with these people ...
No more tears ...
No more arguing ...
No more being accused of ruining THEIR Christmas ...
No more feeling left out of their stupid banter ...
No more hearing "I'll tell you later" ...
No more lies ...
No more being told "you're rude," "you're selfish," etc. ...
No more hearing "you do this every year" ...
No more trying to explain how we deaf people feel left out and hate
    going to family get-togethers ...
No more hearing them say "yes I do understand what you are going
    through" when they aren't deaf themselves ...
No more!

Pilgrimage

I slept all the way back
on the train from DC to Chicago.
The summer rains started again.

I'm returning.
There is a yes, now.
I'm headed
back to my life, paused.

Before, I couldn't see how
to keep traveling onwards
the same old way:

living on scraps
of words, scraps
of relationships,
hearing people.

So when I got an email
inviting me to visit
Gallaudet, I'd taken the
late train from Chicago,
destination, DC.

I'm returning.
I know how, now.

Cocooned in my train seat, I'm rocked
past scenes I later think I dreamed:
water rising, houses flooded, cars
slipped sideways into surprise rivers.
It's Harpers Ferry, then Cumberland,
a long dream through a green
sleeping Pennsylvania.

A midnight sigh in Elyria, Ohio,
bags handed off the train.
A woman quick walking,
a silent voice to a waiting man.
Street lamps lean in like tired strangers,
cupped light in their hands.
In my dreams, I'm still signing,
shaping the signs of remembered
conversations. Back and forth.
Real conversations I don't
have to lipread anymore.

At a gathering in Takoma Park,
we all sit in a well-lit circle,
balancing beers
between legs,
plates presented on knees,
hunching a shoulder,
curving the air between our bodies.

From one side of the circle,
there's a question for me,
Specifically. My mind,
tired and overwhelmed
with joy, can't give his question
a beginning, middle, or end.
But I know it's for me.

Instead, his hands blur,
as though we were in a pool,
Marco Polo, and all I can
feel, with my eyes shut, is the pull
of the water around my neck. I feel
the waves trembling to me
from where I know where he is.

Again, please.

Kristen Harmon

I tell him, my hands stumbling.
He nods, waits for me, in the deep end,
his arms skimming the surface,
in slow circles, Keeping afloat.
Sure. No problem.

It's that gasping fall into the water
I remember most when the train
pulls into Chicago's Union Station.
The moment in between words.
I feel my voice caught in my throat.

I cough, rehearsing
memorized shapes of teeth and
tongue and air.
How to breathe in
when drowning.

Remember how this feels, my speech
therapist had said, placing my hand
on her throat, humming. *Listen*. I nod,
wanting to please her. I turned up the
volume on my hearing aid, but
it's nothing at all. Just more
fire engine ice cream baseball.

I need the verbs,
I need the moves,
the hands
reaching out for me,
my hands in reply,
the laughs,
the love.

In my dreams, I travel from house to
house, slipping through the foundations,
swimming out through attics, trying

before my breath bubbles out,
to find the one

where all the lights
are on, the doors wide open,
the kitchen full of people
chatting and laughing,

the one where, at night,
I throw a quilt
over the bed and rest,
my fingers skimming
familiar shapes.

Perfect Moons

('twas in a dream)
I had walked up the stairs of the
Hall Memorial Building
in the crisp autumn air and saw standing there
a tall, lanky gentleman—about twenty—with a red and white cane.
I saw that he was lost
          so I asked him, slowly,
            if he needed help.
     He removed his sunglasses to show two
         mature cataracts,
      one blue and one milky white,
        that were culpable for
         stealing his sight.
Anyway, he accepted my help,
and we walked on through
         the long halls with the shaking lights
          I dropped him off to his class,
     and he said "thank you" with the grace of a king
          and he looked back at me,
           saying nothing more but
           looking back with those
           two perfect moons.

Heartbreak's Function

A heart's eternal song is the heartbeat,
so too beats the heart's eternal questions: Who am I? Whom do I love?
Who will love me? Am I even worthy of such love?
If logic is a grafted flower, love is a picturesque rosebush:
So pretty, you think! How sharp are the yellows,
pure the whites, deep and warm the oranges, and—fiery and mean the
    reds—
So short on time, or else you'd stop. But how piercing and painful
    would it be to be struck by a thorn!
As life goes on, as you grow ... it becomes tiring, this gardening for
    love,
looking for that perfect rose—a perfect love, an imperfect person for
    an imperfect you.
Some never grow, and embrace a periodicity of love: as though it were
    a sinister sine or a cruel cosine, never-ending,
always curving tortuously—delighting in the maximas and mourning
    in the minimas.
Growth and maturity are not immutable forces of time but rather
    effects of engaging with it—not letting seconds tick by
meaninglessly, but infusing every minute with meaning, and every
    hour with its own eternity.
The heart's song may not be so eternal, for doesn't it always end with
    the symphony of asystole?

Elegy for My Spoon Collection

It began in Arizona,
a souvenir from a tourist shop,

a picture of a saguaro on its head.
I don't know why; I was eight years old;

rocks and shells had lost their sheen.
Years later, the display case brimmed

with silver, bronze, imitation gold
from Key West, the Grand Canyon, Big Sur.

After each slot filled up, I kept
stuffing it, laying spoons on their sides,

that tumbled out each time I opened
the glass door, clinking against the hardwood.

In my twenties, I donated this collection;
I don't know why; could be I prided myself

on being a minimalist.
One of them was not a souvenir.

It was a friend's, who used it
to stir his tea. Before I left

his country, we held each other
as if it was for the last time.

They Don't See Me

I escape the adults
to my top bunk,
yank out my hearing aids—

the yellowing pink molds
reek of ear wax and are hot
and slick with summer.

The silence and cool air
                         bring relief.

But then the cabin's screen door grinds
open and shivers shut in the breeze,
Val and Nina laughing, stomping in.

I feel all this in the small of my back,
the particular way the bed vibrates,
the movements of their shadows.

They don't see me and I don't see them,
but on the walls their hands make
ominous animals.

An owl looms.
               Then a bat.
                      And a wolf.

The CRISPR Scientist

Against the lab's fluorescent chill,
    needle on the dish of Cas-9 liquid,
        I pull the plunger.

The barrel reddens,
    filling, filling. Last week,
        #2162's claws pinched my arm

as I stuck its hairy ear,
    filled its sad deformity with brightness.
        O reader,

the experiment failed!
    #2162 didn't flinch when I clapped,
        still could not hear.

Now #2163 squirms,
    hot fur prickling my palms.
        I lift the needle to its ear and pull—

Deafness Sestina

You order
    me to salute the mouth's blur
        with which I can knit
    only a semblance of pattern.
You bury my jaw
    in apologies, each one sorrier
        than the next. "Sorry, I'm
    deaf," I say, unable to understand you. "Deaf?"
Panic mounting in your eyes, I think of Keats—
    of uncertainties, mysteries, doubts,
        of a videoed MRI of a woman's mouth
    her weird white tongue

walled by black air and white shell-lips.
    She's a mollusk tonguing
        a dark sea,
    a strange moon whose crust blurs,
unblurs as it swallows blackbirds,
    unswallows. You doubt
        the power of the improvised dance.
    Order me to tug taut your mouth into patterns
until I follow. "Yes,
    I'm deaf,"
        my words blurrier than yours.
    I'm sorry

I'm not sorry.
    In deafness uncertainty is a given,
        but you want me certain, to tongue
    my words down smooth.
But I break each word until it is deaf,
    until an estranged one flies out,
        until it is one your world can't readily blur
    back into recognition.

I wish you'd live with my body, this non-pattern.
    It's okay
        to doubt

    the shape of things. It takes faith to doubt
what seems certain.
    I'm sorry
        to watch you squirm
    against the heavy pattern
of normalcy. You're afraid of living with so many
        unknowns to tongue.
    Just feel your way around.
When my husband and I have sex, we are a blur
    of moonlight and the darkest parts of night.
        We're the deafest

parts. When I take out my hearing aids to sleep, the deaf
    part wakes up. It's the same part
        you listen to at night, the doubt
    suddenly cast on what's real, the dream your brain wants to
    pursue.
What is it about hearing that makes one reject the blur?
    When the hearing part of you wakes up
        you can't continue the dream. You must be sorry
    the mind won't accommodate more disorder.
You curl your tongue
    around the day's affairs, get on your feet,
        begin walking the familiar pattern.

I'm tired of the pattern,
    tired of always apologizing
        for the part I can't change: the deaf
    part. I'm tired of
forcing the tongue
    into all the right grooves.
        I'm tired of feeling your doubt.
I'm sorry I'm deaf?

No, I'm not sorry.
Here, in deafness,
　　we're all pulse and blur,

　all tongue that wants to evade a pattern,
to blur and turn deaf
　　and doubt and not be sorry.

.

J.S. HOSSEN

T' Ls'tn *

Y'' m'st try t' hear
Try t' b'lnd 'n w'th th' cr'wd
W r s srry.

Wht a tr'g'dy
T be n'ly hlf h'rng
To se bt nt hear.

Wht I se you cn't
Wht I hear you cn't
Th t'lnt t hld cn'vr'st'n

Evry'thng tks time
I t'rn th' hearing aids d'wn sw'mpd by th' s'nd
Lt'thr'gc t' th' s'nd
Dis'b'ld by th' s'nd

L'vng 'n th' t'thr of p't'nce
As I str'ggl' t' l'st'n

* There are different types of hearing loss and that the writer has a rare
  type that affects vowel sounds at first, making it hard to comprehend
  speech. It's also known as "Cookie Bite Hearing Loss."

The Housemates

Is anything anyone's fault?

Should they have been more courteous?

Should they have shut their mouths?

People only know what they know.

Until they know any better.

But if you're too courteous, you'll forget to be courteous to yourself!

J.S. HOSSEN

Haiku

Drinking Tequila.
On a dull Tuesday morning.
Nothing else to do.

I've been making way.
For a constant daydreamer.
He's with the fairies.

How long can one stare?
Into a wall, to a door.
Sucked into abyss.

The regions of hell.
Conceived to those who know it.
The bottomless pit.

The magic glitter.
The fast cars on the freeway.
Yes, we can hear you.

I'm here, but I'm there.
When I left how would I know.
They've never even seen me.

The heater is on.
The dog sits by at close range.
As it warms its balls.

Slowgaze confusion.
Fleeting feelings of stoned love
Hazy days indeed.

He waits, lasagne.
In the oven, lasagne.
Lockdown lasagne.

Sober addiction.
He was her rehab romance.
A warmth in the night.

J.S. HOSSEN

Lost at Sea

My friends: lost at sea
I point them to the lighthouse
But their eyes cannot see
From their perils, atrocities
Drugged up to lifelessness
No lifeboat would take them
Numbed and subdued
Pillars of their mind lost to the tides
Memories fade, decay
Cursed by their shadows
Too painful to bring to bay

Ode to Saturn

The cosmos,	your iris.
The big bang,	life in view.
A filter,	masking undesirables.
A black screen,	hiding time robbery.
It all evaporates,	like your memories.
Your life,	its entropy.
Your clock,	the final tick-tock.

Borrowed Silence

Yesterday, I picked up my six-year old daughter from summer day camp in the late afternoon. On the car ride home, she asked me to play the song " The Circle Game." While driving, I managed to download it from Apple Music on my iPhone and hit play. I smiled guiltily with pride at accomplishing this dangerous move while operating a moving car. This song is one of my favorites—one of the few songs that is clear enough for me to hear the lyrics and repetitive enough for me to have memorized them. All the women in our family adore this song.

However, when I looked in the rear view mirror to see if my daughter was singing along like I was, I saw a very distressed young face. "I can't hear it," she cried.

Since she often wishes for media to play at a louder volume than I do, I turned the volume on my iPhone up to the maximum. Still she protested that she could not hear it.

"It's playing at full volume," I told her.

"But I can't hear it," she cried back. By now, the tone of her voice was starting to teeter on the verge of panic. Trying to pay attention to both the road and her cries, I handed the phone itself back to her in the backseat. She held it up to her ear, fiddled with the volume control, and handed it back to me. By this point she was on the verge of tears.

"Why can't you hear it?" I asked in confusion. To me, the song was playing loud and clear. "What's wrong, sweetie?"

She burst into tears for real now so I pulled the car off the road and parked so I could turn around and talk to her more easily. She kept repeating in an agitated voice, "I can't hear it, I can't hear ..." and sobbing frantically.

I said to her, "But you can hear me fine right now, so there is nothing wrong with your hearing."

She just sobbed in response.

I turned back around and stared at my phone thoughtfully. Suddenly, I remembered the time last week when her headphones had been connected via Bluetooth to our television, which meant that we couldn't hear anything through the air. I remembered that my new cochlear implant connected via Bluetooth to an app on my phone that allowed me to control the volume level of the implant. Perhaps it had also made music played on the phone stream directly to the implant?

I quickly pulled up settings and turned off Bluetooth. Instantly, Lena looked up in surprise, her cheeks wet with tears, as the song filled the car. I explained what had happened to her as we slowly finished the drive home. It took her most of the drive to stop sniffling, dry her tears, and enjoy the song.

When we pulled into the driveway, she hopped out and ran inside to tell my wife the story. The next day on the way to camp again, she told her carpool friend the story.

I know that this is her way of processing the fear she felt for those 10-15 minutes when she truly thought that my reality had become her own.

The Rock

I've been carrying around a sharp piece of rock in one fist since
toddlerhood.

If I held it gently, I could still do most things in life … with one fist
closed.

But if I squeezed tightly, the blood ran between my fingers and
dripped and dripped and dripped …

I have clear memories of trying to show previous therapists my rock.

The responses varied:

"Ouch, that looks dangerous and it's hurting you. You should put that
down."

"Why are you still carrying around something you picked up so very
long ago?"

"Well, that's an interesting rock but look at these smooth ones!
Wouldn't one of these feel better than that old spiky thing?"

"If you took the time, you could smooth out those jagged edges on your
own."

So I closed up my fist and went back to life.

Then one day I met a new therapist.

After a few months, they gently commented on the fist that was always
closed.

So against my own better judgment, I held the jagged rock up to the
Zoom camera, bloodstains and all.

"Ooooh, look at that," they said. "I love how the light catches it at this angle and makes it appear translucent."

"I've never seen another rock like it. I understand completely why you'd want to hold on to this. Thank you for sharing it with me."

I hurriedly closed my fist again and changed the topic.

I did notice that my paperwork seemed less frequently bloodstained as the months went by, but we rarely discussed my rock.

And then, as they shifted the location of their laptop one day for a session, I noticed a large bowl of smooth polished rocks sitting on a shelf in the background.

"I didn't know you had a bunch of rocks in your life," I mumbled.

"Yes," they replied with a smile. "Or rather, I do now. They weren't always that smooth and shiny, though, nor have they always lived here in my office. I used to carry them around with me, too."

"Speaking of which, how is your beautiful rock doing?"

I looked down at my fist as I uncurled the frozen fingers. To my astonishment, the rock wasn't there.

I must have dropped it somewhere, I thought as I started to panic. Who would I be without my rock?

I scrambled around and finally found it sitting on the floor in a corner, its jagged edges shining in the light from the office window.

"It's … here," I said in confusion.

"Would you want to find a place for it in your own office?" asked the therapist.

"Maybe you don't have to carry it with you every day?"

Maybe not, I thought slowly as I flexed my tired fingers.

Maybe not?

Snowflakes

You scamper in snow,
late evening.
The flurries sparkle
as they fall.
Darkness is near.

Branches,
brittle and frozen,
crack. They
crash
around you.

You're fearless.
Deer, rabbits and squirrels
abound.
Your tail dances,
in pursuit.
The
creatures sneak
around,
as if hungry thieves
crawling through the night.

Command

We speak to one another as if
using a same language.
My calm voice soothes you.
You tug the leash.

The snow is soft and shimmers
beneath your oversized paws.
The snow's crust crackles beneath my army boots.
My arm becomes sore,
From the yanking and the pulling.
You, whiny, chase for the deer but
they are as relentless
as a gazelle being hunted down the Sahara.

And I speak for both of us.
I say commands.
You respond
and you let up
whilst we follow the trail back,
The deer,
now elusive,
left behind as
if abandoned treasures.

The Red Dress

It's vintage, you say
As you hold the red cocktail dress
up before you in front of a mirror.
Red is my country. This dress is mine.
Merlot.
Excuse me?
Merlot. Not red. The dress is merlot.
Your eyes turn dismissive.
And it's vintage, you say. And
I must have this.

We glance at the price tag.
I move away.
Not a problem, you say,
your hand stopping me by my arm.
I'll pay you back.
The store gets busier and
The door opens, closes, and opens.

In a single movement,
you rip a tear,
along the sleeve.
Sequins scatter on the floor.

That shall get me twenty percent off,
at least!
I go with you among the aisles
and I become lost so I just
follow the red sequined dress,
slung over your shoulder.
You turning and smiling my way.
It's your teeth, I most remember
About that day.
And not about the tear.

WILLIAM T. VANDEGRIFT, JR.

It's your teeth having been painted
I won't forget.
Your patriotic smile, a bright array
aglow for the holiday.
A luminous smile of radium
spread widely,
with a shiny sparkle
that not even a sequined dress can bring.

Wings

There on the bed.
Like a butterfly, caught
Within the folds of death,
Aflutter.
Lacking a wing.
A bright, lovely, blue wing.
Like one belonging to an aging dowager
Ladened with Ostrich tails and boas.
Corn silk and rouge.
Airbrushed wigs and wings.

A bottle of sea glass,
greenish all the way around,
with blue in it.
Glass shards.
now round and soft,
circle the round bottom.
It has been waiting for you.

You cannot take your eye off it.
Uneven holes are punched
around the lid,

You,
net in air,
in the fields
While I
sit with the jar.
in shade.
And I watch the butterflies tossing
themselves
against the jar's glass.

You come back with more.

To make room,
we'd let a few go
and kept the prettiest ones.

In morning,
out of bed I am.
I cannot find you.
Then I do. You are by the toilet, jar open.
You're motionless.
I poke you with a pencil.
You begin to crumble.
I retrieve the lost wing,
from the pillow I left it on,
Feathery and gray with swirls of purple,
and I place this wing, already flaking,
inside the jar
And I tightly secure the lid.

The destruction of beauty
and of my youth
come to one.
I artfully begin to scrape the loveliness away
from along my shoreline
until nothing,
absolutely nothing
beautiful about me is left behind
to be admired or taken.

Me as a Color

Blue.

I am Dark Periwinkle Blue.
I am a combination color. I am blue, I am violet.

Sultry but true. Deep through and through
To the cell, the mitochondria, the telomere.

I am energy. I am ageless. I am of all ages
Before birth in spirit, and after transitions.

I am deep teal to the soul.

I am the bright, unusual blue to the feminine.
Masculine focus and energy blended.
Loving myself. Drawing in the other.

Deep as the night sky at dusk. Sunrise just after darkness.
The awakening azure teal emerges from dark from the glittering stars.
Shares its deep, dark wisdom with the coming daylight
Deep as the ocean, the blue-black sea.

Viewing a Monochrome Carot

The air is a nonreflective black draped over water
The water, too, is black
Silver ink pens an arc, drawing eyes to land

There the trees should be bursting greens, alive
But they, too, are black
Logs, rocks float water in slate
Roots hanging from trees dangle in black

From high aerial angle, buff color made from light illuminates
A small girl flat on stomach, on the immense, black forest floor
Light reflects her skin, book pages, blouse,
Curled toes at the ends of upturned feet

Far-off distance casts light on yellow brick-shaped rocks
Shaft of birch in paint-by-numbers whites and grays
Up high and far, pale blue sky, small white cloud

Form small and strong finds kinship far off
In yellow, blue, dappled gray and white

Still, the massive nonreflective black
Surrounds translucent living light

A Nod to Camus: "In winter I discover an invincible summer."

That's really me right now.
The obsession has been lifted. The compulsion simply gone.
Today I notice freedom. To move. To assemble.
Dishes and plates, silver and glass.
Into the dishwasher, at last.

Filling and sorting and stacking, put away.
Then to fill up, over and over again.
I act.

I reach out to my plates.
They are gathered together and shelved.
I'm trying to find a rhyme but that's for deep meanings.
These are just dishes, forks, glass bowls and cups.
But how scattered they've been.
How unruly they'd became.
How refusing they are to budge.

Covered with pages of the *New York Times* daily.
With Sondheim and Vindman, Fiona and Misha.
All piled on, there's new order in the body politic, in plates.

I devour every article.
Foreign nations or artists or foods or big tech machinations.

I now choose.

I say no.

How decisive I've become,
Not chained to the printed pages.

Upward they float.
A dish appears.

Removed and rising.
Lifted up, dropped down, and stored.

Dad why are you gone?

Dad why are you gone?
Was it because I clung too much on,
the sleeve of your crewneck wool sweater?
Or because I couldn't hear the crowd
When the Miami Dolphins scored?

Did I drag my feet too much?
To where it sounded like razor blades on a chalkboard?
Or when I ran across the black asphalt road,
Without looking both ways?
Are these the reasons for your absence?

Was it because I placed second place in the Academic Bowl Regionals?
While you never passed the seventh grade.
Washing cars for a living,
While I became a wordsmith?
Is this why you rarely visited or called?

I made and kept many promises to grandma after she died from cancer,
While you never showed up to her funeral.
Or that I would hug my mother with care,
While you treated her like a filthy ragdoll.
Do you keep your distance because I'm a better man?

Your reasons are always shrouded in mystery,
Nor do I know whether you love me or not.
All I truly know is that one question,
I asked myself when I lay down my head at night:
Dad, why are you gone?

Audiogram

They sat me in a room
Strapping wires that transforms
Into snakes from Medusa's head
Giant headphones clamp down on my ears
Blasting penetrating waves

Eaaaooouunnhhh

Eaaaooouunnhhh

Eaaaooouunnhhh

Eaaaooouunnhhh

Eaaaooouunnhhh

Eaaaooouunnhhh
Years of saying the same words
Over, over and over again
Say the word apple
Ap-uh
Say the word house
Hou-ziz
Say the word Hot-dog
Hot-dawg
Using all the tests to construct a mapping
Guiding my education, life and communication
My own Guantanamo Bay

Exiled

Every brush stroke emerged a smile
Calm and serenity painted upon a canvas
Smoothing hands upon ceramic clay
Originated from the passionate heart
Painstaking sketches from a pencil
Forms shapes and lines of laborious love
But sounds from within my cochlea began to fade
Forced eruptions of confusion and chaos from the silence
My craft and abilities soon dissolved
As the directions were obscure
The pedagogue exiled the deafened artist

Collisions

Fireflies
They light up skies
Smashing into windshields
Blinking out from our memories
Lights off

Whitetail
Headlights, wide eyes
Careening metal death trap
Bone crushing, blood curdling bleating
Road kill

Snapper
Crawling homeward
A slow moving target
Swerving, incoming manslaughter
Splattered

Red Hawk
Scanning highway
An explosion of fur
Wings spread, skydiving for fast food
Near miss

Green Frogs
A rainy night
Hundred amphibians
Asphalt graveyard, rubber demons
Flattened

Grandma

One moment we're laughing,
In the yard digging up worms
Aluminum cans filled with squigglies
Our hearts fill with joy
Hard to breathe
Your laughter ceased
You and the oxygen tank watch from afar

Up in the attic, wonders of art
Autumn colors on canvas
The brush swish and swoosh
I dribble little birds, flying high
Soon, dust collects, acrylics dry
Attic stairs too daunting to climb

Always playing "make-believe"
Shop owner, zookeeper and silly games
Dramatic like Mozart with a Spielberg flair
Eventually, everyone plays pretend
Hiding your trip to the abyss

Awoken to a world without you
Told the angels took you to heaven
You've become a butterfly
Beautification of freedom
Witnessed Grandpa in distress
Opening and closing your casket

Nostalgia

Love is like pay phones,
Forever disconnected.
Memories fading,
From the strips of VHS.
Pieces of my heart are littered,
Like a shattered vinyl.
Attempts to keep the romance alive,
But met death like a Tamagotchi.
You once said I was your baby …
Discarded me like a Beanie Baby.
Stomped my heart into salsa,
Flavored with buttered nostalgia.

Doneness of You
In memory of John F. Dunsmore 11/22/1964–8/18/2019

You were not present
    grasping for moments
    arriving with scared naiveness
You were oppressed
    the whiteness
    the emptiness from silence
You were suffering
    heavy breaths grasping for air
    rushed feet
You were not heard
    the coldness
    the touches seeking for answers
You did not get soothed
    tears a'flowing
    hearts violently crushed
You did not breathe
    stomach holding on to the fleshy pieces from the heart
    squeezes for connection
You signed ILY, then faded away to sleep
    communiques fading away
    grasping for time
You never woke up
    drops turned into unchartered rivers
    shattered goodbyes
You left abruptly
    tension of eternity gone
    forever, no more
holding his hand with ours.

Chronolanguage

Mechanical devices poking our nerves
some permanent, some lurking
stressor in the body creating discomfort
ongoing, never-ending, obsessing over
trauma leeched in our brain
triggers sucked in with diseases of squeezes!

Speech, spondee words, amplification
cymbals clapping, rewarded
dark glowing eyes from the simian
laughing, mocking, bullying, brainwashing
the lies in my brain that hearing knows it all!

Effort to communicate, none
can't do things, not allowed
actions, patronized, minimized
rejections, all discriminatory
deafness, oh my, what a tragedy!

Hands moving along with shapes
aura filled with colorful articulation
coded with clarity to connect with others
native, near-native, intermediate, beginner
Uniqueness of internalized segregation occurs!

Hierarchy, families, schools, friends, intellectualism
not hearing enough
not deaf enough
from birth to now
criticism targeting cultural appropriateness not appropriation!

Testimonies, unique obstacles
accepting differences
controversies create connections

assimilation strengthens
the truth of our own souls filled by chronolanguage!

Visualmetaphor

Characterized by its own philosophical depth
accented the exploration of our own competency to connect

mixture of complex sentiments within our core
through its own usage of repetitive habits

destiny's setting motivates how life became skilled
discovering the direct you

sentiments skillfully dealt with by living passionately
living truthfully with sensitivity and awareness

the openly spark of hands and heart visually stimulating
life's gifts and journey's bumps

creation of enoughness, its own integrity by assuming our own place
by being present, there, for the eyes to bypass peacefully

togetherness demands its serving others to love with conviction
blinks, thoughts, and pauses all creatively combined to convoy you

no wrong moment to describe what is metaphorically personal
serves its purpose no more, let it go

forming life's pain due to its past of never expressing up again
because of its truth

my chapter, closing with breaths through the soft skins of my blinds.

Riot of Rainbows

clothes concede to conformity in the men's section since
basic black & bolder blue both buttress binary of gender

though my soul seeks sequins, for trans folks
on both sides of the border this is a dangerous time

still daily i don my rainbow amour as resistance,
a rebellion against the binary as well as a show of pride

pushing back against stigmatizing stereotypes of deficit
where behind the ear hearing aids are automatically boring & banal

with purple casings, pink filters & molds with glitter embedded
my behind the ear hearing aids are a riot of rainbows

Colour as Reclamation

my carefully casual question: lips form round c shape, draw out the
    vowel of o
tongue on roof of my mouth for the middle consonant then a hard
    sharp sound for the r
an example of oralism, audism & phonocentrism operating in
    synchronicity

(r remains a tricky inconstant consonant to pronounce,
trying to be a helpful older sibling, i taught my baby brother the wrong
    way to say r
among my hearing family this remains a funny childhood story not an
    oralist outcome)

brown brows bunch as the young audiologist repeats that word
as a hearing specialist, one would think they would understand the
    simple question
yet they pair it with others my mandatorily meticulously trained mind
    is too tired to fill in

(i catch 'skin' & 'tones,' the subtle side-step & shuffle that speaks the
    unspeakable
decades later i will learn how to discuss this confidently, directly in
    relation to disability
using terms of DisCrit & LatDisCrit; now Canadian politeness keeps
    me silent)

now i save the spoons of my spoken words for the most pressing
    priority
still careful but less casual, i repeat my request more firmly adding a
    gesture
emphasizing heteronormative masculinity in case my voice is too soft
    or too slurred

(i know, my entire team of specialists knows treatment for my
    multiple disabilities
causes dry mouth that impacts my voice yet 'phonocentrism' is a
    unknown word
meaning advocating for written communication & being honoured is
    decades away)

after more meaningless mouth sounds audiologists' arguments appear
    to end
with wheel of colourful options for filters & behind the ear hearing
    aids before me
i think of pride yet audiologist states the models which fit adults are
    intended for children

(colours were never an option when I was a child, now nuances of
    audism mean
children can choose colours as parents pick pamphlets promoting
    phonocentrism
while adults like myself must apparently advocate for colourful
    choices)

the molds are another siege against the fortress of ableism & its
    nuances
again, I ask my carefully casual question about colours & again the
    audiologist
radiates reluctance in their jaw, their tense posture & the new line on
    their forehead

(it is probably in their tone of voice too but i have never been able to
    tell tones of voice
my many mandatory speech therapists loudly lamented & deemed this
    a 'failure'
decades later I will learn to the accurate term, a failure of 'compulsory
    able-bodiedness')

i temper my expression to politeness & focus on selecting fabulous &
    queer colours

carefully chosen colourful casing, filters & molds as a rainbow armour
one i will put on with pride before going out to battle with all ableist
    nuisances

Accessibility, Elsewhere

shocked & surprised fingers fumble with the remote
seeing sign language interpreter covering politics on local news
shown same size non-Deaf announcer in an example of Deaf equity

ceaseless crash of the Caribbean Sea makes my oralist upbringing
    irrelevant
as waves overwhelm the volume of my meticulously shaped speech
yet my explanation of 'Deaf' is not met with phonocentrism or audism

Deaf skills of communication; using paper & pen or thumbing out a
    text
are required not requested or recommended in this elsewhere space,
a small slice of island paradise, northern nations would do well to
    emulate

So odd how strange women on the street

insisted on telling me how I must be
so inspiring to others. What had I done?
Their dull red lipstick circled the words
as they spoke, always smiling as if I should
not be taking things so hard because I was
such a good boy, is that right?
I shifted from one foot to another.
Must I really lipread these women
who had felt it their mission to lift me
a bit closer to the heavens?
Did the thingamajigs in my ears
have that much power, possibly
a holy relic? Was I supposed to bless
their kindhearted encouragement?
Were my hearing aids a miracle?
How was beatification supposed to work?
Was I supposed to be a saint in training?
I wanted to rip out my earmolds,
its tips cherry-topped with caramel wax,
and offer them up like communion wafers,
a choice reliquary to inspire them
into never tapping my shoulder again.

M-e-r-i-t {Badges-Down-Across} Sash
after Juliette Low Gordon (1860–1927)

[*in ASL gloss*]

Daisy you-gullible wow
Everything you-read believe
If print, authority have
Same-same God bless
First page Bible shine-shine

Age 25 earache-left-ear
You-read n-i-t-r-a-t-e silver pain dissolve can
You demand doctor inject point-ear
Happen what
Eat-up e-a-r-d-r-u-m
That noise point-ear you-hear last finish

Later wedding day g-r-a-i-n r-i-c-e
Stuck right-ear
You never notice travel honeymoon
Ear feel-like fire
Doctor try pluck r-i-c-e
Accident e-a-r-d-r-u-m hole
Scratch pull right-ear last thing you-hear finish

Late-deafen, talk-up-up-up
Why? Lipread can't
You fascinating one-way talker
Then you try electric horn
If not connect right, f-e-e-d-b-a-c-k awful

Age 51 idea pop-up
Set-up group girls learn-learn skills
Same R-o-b-e-r-t B-a-d-e-n—P-o-w-e-l-l establish Boy-Scouts
Mothers trust daughters with you why?
Yourself G-o-r-d-o-n therefore lady elegant-elegant

Age 66 get what? T-e-l-e-g-r-a-m
Board-of-directors write what
" " You not only first Girl Scout but best Girl Scout champ!
Proud heart-inflate
T-e-l-e-g-r-a-m where? Jacket breastpocket you-bury with

Deaf children now? They look-at people
Talking-out-loud not-understand
They learn task list progress become older
Realize list that worthless
Daisy, inform-you no-one send t-e-l-e-g-r-a-m finish

His nasal voice grated on my nerves.

I did not like how he tried to answer in class.
  (*Oh, him again?!?*)
He wore the ugliest shirts.
  (*Ugly, ugly, ugly!*)
His hand-me-down terry socks shouted cheap.
  (*Athletic socks are better.*)
He deserved to stand over there by the brick wall
  (*Just look at him!*)
where the kids played Nerf football.
  (*He can't even play. Oh, man.*)
One day he kept popping into my mirror.
  (*Who are you?*)
I razored him with names.
  (*You're such a crybaby! Yeah, you.*)
I bruised him a rosary of tears.
  (*Must he cry again? YES.*)
He was such a runt.
  (*Runt runt runt!*)
I blunted his ability to cry in class.
  (*You know we're watching.*)
He was much better off silent.
  (*Such a weird voice!*)
His face showed no cracks.
  (*You can stop crying, ya know.*)
Not even a smile.
  (*What do you got against us?*)
He was a perfect statue.
  (*That brick wall sure suits ya.*)
Day and night he stands,
  (*Oh yeah, we're having fun over here.*)
never speaking from the pedestal,
  (*Will you just stop staring at me?*)
his eyes always weathering
  (*Gosh, don't you ever smile at all?*)

the grief-aches from my bones
    (*Why are you moving so slow?*)
each time I shave my face.
    (*Wait—just* who *are you?*)
How I never raised my hand
    (*Can't I just snicker for once?*)
to answer his unasked question
    (*What's our name?*)
why I had hated myself so.

If My Eyes Were Dandelion

I would not see the land as filled with weeds
but creatures seen equal to any flower, even

if crowned in butter gold and feather white,
high-collared and laced in mustardy greens,

therefore beautiful and worthy of existence
much as the tall trees that guard the periphery

of the woods wherever we tender our presence.
We would not feel ashamed of being, as exactly we are,

of viewing the landscape a little differently,
of feeling sad from losing so many friends

whisked from dawn to death by the wind.
We would not feel so afraid of such a prospect

even when we've aged into seedheads,
perfect haloes of wisdom and ache

with not yet a loss of follicle.
We would sense how we were not alone,

how perhaps we aren't supposed to be grit in the eyes
of anyone, but if we indeed are, well, then,

we shall be grateful to have annoyed
for it means that we had mattered

even if only for an eye-blink. Wind, hurry.
We await our turn in the glorious sun.

When the Moon Took My Name

I had no name.
Only ache.
Until the Moon called me forward,
laid my sorrow in a silver bowl,
and carved a name
from shadowlight.
Not man.
Not woman.
Something older.
Something sky-shaped.
My silence made sound
in her glow.
She did not speak—
but I understood:
"You belong."
She named me
Dreamwalker.
Two-Spirit.
Talk With Hands.
And I remembered
the shape of myself.

Feather in the Wind

Before the Rainbow Warrior, it rests—
both hands cupped,
holding silence like a sacred flame.
With honor and a smile,
he takes the seat of the storyteller.
Guardians of land and sea
gather in the mist,
spirits whisper through moss-laced trees,
and ancestors circle like wind.
He is not alone.
In Quinault's shadowed stillness,
he walks with bare feet,
guided by the Red Road,
with the Great Creator
breathing through the roots.
Talk with Hands,
with his Blue Dream Feather Quill,
writes not with ink,
but with vibrations.
Stories rise from soil and song,
each one a gift,
each one a step.
Feather in the wind—
his name,
his oath,
his truth.

Hands Like Wingbeats

These hands are never still.
They do not rest,
they rise.
Each sign
is a feather beating against silence,
each pause
a prayer to wind.
My language
is movement,
is air,
is lightning without thunder.
And when I speak,
sky leans in—
because it recognizes
its own.

In the Silence, I Speak

My voice is so loud
it needs to hush.
My hands dance,
each gesture a thunderclap
in a soundless storm.
I do not fear
what I cannot hear.
I see no fear,
speak no fear—
I become the wind.
They say trees do not speak.
But I do.
With body, breath,
and the sacred shape
of signing fingers,
I speak my spirit.
You call it silence.
I call it creation.
Unseen,
unheard,
but undeniable.

Firekeeper's Daughter

They said the flame would destroy me.
They said silence was safer.
But I was born with smoke in my breath
and red coals in my blood.
I was never meant to tend the fire.
I am the fire—
the smoke,
the ember,
the howl at dusk.
You may not see me coming.
But I'll leave ash that glows.
I am the firekeeper's daughter—
the one who writes in sparks.

Just Smile

They asked for my voice.
I gave them my hands.
They looked confused.
So I gave them my body—
each movement a sentence.
Each breath a verse.
Still, they asked for sound.
I smiled.
I had already told them
everything.
They didn't hear.
But the moon did.
And that was enough.

Charlie Ainsworth is a Deaf writer and filmmaker based in Minneapolis. His work spans poetry, satire, and screenwriting, often exploring Deaf identity and experience. He's the founder of Angry Deaf People, a movement in Deaf cinema, and is developing Project Hotbed, a long-term funding initiative to sustain Deaf-led films. When not writing or plotting his next story, Charlie is raising two Deaf daughters and stirring up good trouble in the world of Deaf arts. [angrydeafpeople.com]

Karen Christie (she/her/ella) (name sign KC) is a Deaf white, sighted woman who grew up in California and made her way into the Deaf community in her teenage years. At the National Technical Institute for the Deaf/Rochester Institute of Technology, she taught Deaf cultural studies/English. She presently works at Deaf Refugee Advocacy. Some of her poetry has appeared in *Wordgathering*, *Nine Mile Magazine*, and *Deaf Lit Extravaganza*.

S. Leigh Ann Cowan is a white, deaf, queer ciswoman who was born on a Tuesday morning. She holds a master's degree in Deaf Studies (Gallaudet University '22) and both a bachelor's and master's degrees in English Literature and Language (Henderson State University '18, St. Mary's University TX '20). You can find more about Leigh Ann and her work, especially her passion for deaf representation in fiction. [slacowan.com]

Linda Drattell's two poetry chapbooks, *Remember This Day* (Reader Views Bronze Award) and *The Lighter Side of Horse Manure*, are published by Finishing Line Press. She co-authored *Who Wants to be Friends With a Dragon?* (Dorrance Publishing). Her poetry is published in anthologies and literary magazines; has been reviewed on blogs, podcasts, and news media; and won awards from *Writer's Digest* (second place), *Atlanta Review* Poetry International Grand Prize (finalist), and C&R Press Poetry Prize (longlisted).

Martha Ellen lives alone in an old Victorian house on a hill on the Oregon coast. Retired social worker. History of social justice activism. MFA. Poems and prose published in various journals and online forums. She writes to process her wild life.

Kristen Harmon, born deaf to hearing parents, is now a professor of English at Gallaudet University. She also is a communications specialist and executive management senior advisor for Gallaudet University Press. She has published short stories and creative nonfiction and is also an editor of multiple collections of creative writing written by Deaf people. Additionally, she has published scholarly articles on a range of topics, from Deaf literature to narrative methodologies to Deaf bilingualism in education, and so on.

Abby Haroun is a writer, editor, and poet with an MFA in creative writing from the University of Baltimore and a PhD in English from Morgan State University. She has roots in West Africa and England, where she spent her early years. Abby is a recipient of the Adele V. Holden Creative Writing Excellence Award. Her poetry was displayed in the renowned Guggenheim Museum's *Ekphrasis in Air* exhibit.

Alex Hawkins (Talk With Hands) is a Deaf Two-Spirit storyteller and poet whose work weaves ancestral memory, dream language, and spiritual symbolism. Rooted in the Quinault Rainforest and Deaf culture, Alex crafts tales that blend nature's whispers, inner healing, and vivid imagination.

J.S. Hossen grew up in Perth, Western Australia. They have a rare form of hearing loss called "Cookie Bite Hearing Loss." This loss affects the ability to hear mid-range frequencies. Vowel sounds are often difficult to hear, resulting in listening fatigue and misunderstandings. J.S. Hossen was born hearing and started to lose it progressively needing hearing aids by the age of 14. They can occasionally be seen performing spoken poetry in Perth and, in the future, would like to perform in Auslan which they are currently learning. Their favorite poets are Sharon Olds, Emily Dickinson, Charles Bukowski, and John Keats.

Michael Isaacs is a deaf poet from Ramsgate. He started writing poetry in 2019 to channel his grief after his mother died. He is severely deaf and wears bone-anchored hearing aids (BAHAs). Michael, who also has Crohn's and OCD, is an advocate for hidden disability awareness through poetry. He has won multiple poetry slams. Michael has had his poetry featured in local magazines. He is currently working on a poetry anthology about invisible disabilities.

Lilah Katcher's poetry has appeared in *Barrelhouse*, *Postcard Poems and Prose*, *Poetry International*, *Gargoyle*, and *Mollyhouse*. Her flash fiction is included in the anthology *Tripping the Light Fantastic: Weird Fiction by Deaf and Hard of Hearing Writers*. She has an MFA from American University, where she worked as the nonfiction editor for *FOLIO*. Lilah would love to see more ASL poetry translated into English and have her own poetry translated into ASL.

Sarah Katz is a deaf writer in Northern Virginia who experiments across genres. She is the author of *Country of Glass*, a poetry collection published by Gallaudet University Press (2022). Her poetry has been published in *Bear Review*, *Poetry Daily*, and *RHINO Poetry*, among others. She earned a BA in English from the University of Maryland, College Park, and an MFA in Creative Writing from American University. [sarahbeakatz.com]

Jer Loudenback has been Deaf since birth and the only Deaf member in his hearing family. A Washington state native, he moved to Minnesota after retiring as an ASL instructor and teacher of the Deaf. He is actively involved in numerous Deaf organizations, which he enjoys immensely. He has performed ASL poems, but this is Jer's third published work. He has enjoyed this process so much!

Raymond Luczak (Editor) is the Deaf author and editor of 38 books, including *Animals Out-There W-i-l-d: A Bestiary in English and ASL Gloss*, *The Language of Home: Stories,* and *Ironhood: Poems*. His next poetry collection *[Exeunt.]* will appear in the spring of 2026. His work has appeared in *Poetry*, *Prairie Schooner*, and elsewhere. An inaugural Zoeglossia Poetry Fellow, he lives in Minneapolis, Minnesota. [raymondluczak.com]

Thomas Muething is a 2010 and 2014 alumnus respectively of The Ohio School for the Deaf and Gallaudet University. Born hard of hearing, he signed with his late mother and transitioned into the Deaf world in late adolescence. Seattle is home for now. His soul remains in Shepherd Park. "Perfect Moons" was first graded as part of a final activities at Gallaudet University Spring 2011 in an honors class, DC Noir, by Dr. Jennifer L. Nelson and The Rev. Dr. Kirk A. VanGilder.

Cheryl Nichols has been profoundly deaf since birth. She was born in Tulsa, OK, and moved to Seattle, WA when she was five years old. She loves her job as a paraeducator working with deaf students. She enjoys traveling, photographing, reading, and watching the ocean waves for relaxation.

Kris Ringman (they/she) is a Deaf queer author and artist. They write lyrical fiction and poetry inspired by nature, wildlife, and world mythology. They are the author of *Sail Skin: poems* (Handtype Press, 2022) as well as two Lambda Literary Finalist titles: *I Stole You: stories from the fae* (Handtype Press, 2017) and *Makara: a novel* (Handtype Press, 2012), and the editor of *Everyday Haiku: an anthology* (Wandering Muse Press, 2017). Both their fiction and poetry have been nominated for the Pushcart Prize. When they're not writing, painting murals, or making art, they can be found on the ocean or in the mountains. [krisringman.com]

Curtis Robbins has been a poet since he was 14 years old. A minor stroke has prevented him from writing more after 2015. His deafness overshadows the vernacular spoken word. He has worn a cochlear implant since he was over 45 years old which is far better than the hearing aid which he'd worn for over 40 years. Poetry has been his life's work. He's published two poetry collections. He's been married for 52 years with two grown children and three grandchildren.

Prudence Shaw is a person.

Maverick Smith, a D/deaf, queer, trans*, disabled, genderqueer person who has always been interested in social justice and equity. They currently reside on the traditional lands of the Mississaugas of the New Credit in Tkaronto (Toronto). Their poetry and prose focuses on resisting audism and taking pride in their identity as a Deaf person.

Lori Stambler-Dunsmore specializes in collages/photomontages and creative writing. Her creative work was featured at Florida Deaf Art Show, Dyer Arts Center, Expo Metro, Ikouii, Resource Depot, and through art collectives. She was also cast in *Not Another Deaf Story*, a multimedia theater piece. Prior to August 2019, and her evolvement as an artist, Lori was an academic, advocate, public health specialist, administrator at Deaf schools, and a culinary artist. She earned three academic degrees as well as educational and culinary certificates. [IG: @moments_by_lori]

William T. Vandegrift, Jr. lives in between New York City and Philadelphia in bucolic Central New Jersey with his husband, two cats, and a Boxer Shepherd puppy named Dancer. He has developed a passion for pottery. He is busy at work on a novella and a memoir about trauma and grief. He enjoys poetry and monologue-writing. He holds an MFA from Bennington College in Writing and Literature.

Jacob Waring enjoys orbiting the planets of weird fiction, creating tales with a splash of space, mystery, and horror. He is also a freelance journalist. Waring has contributed to the anthologies *Tripping the Tale Fantastic: Weird Fiction by Deaf and Hard of Hearing Writers* and *I'll Tell You Later: Deaf Survivors of Dinner Table Syndrome.*

Mel Whalen, PhD, LP (they/them), is a Deaf, queer, humanistic clinical psychologist who runs a private practice in Michigan. A Fulbright Scholar with an MA in Sign Linguistics, Mel integrates writing into their clinical work as both therapeutic tool and reflective practice. Their work draws from narratives of trauma, disability, identity, parenthood and survivor activism. It lives at the edges of vulnerability and resistance, always seeking the healing power of language to name what was once unspeakable.

Alex Wilhite (Cover Artist), an American artist from Tuscumbia, AL, was raised in St. Louis, MO, began exploring art at age five. He holds a BFA from the University of North Alabama and an MFA from Pratt Institute, Brooklyn, NY. Alex is currently merging art and communication as a Montessouri educator using sign language at the School of the Woods in Houston, Texas. His work is inspired by Minimalism, Tonalism, and the Hudson River School. Known for creating unique pigments and color theories, his tranquil artworks reflect a profound artistic vision, making a significant impact in both the arts and teaching communities. [artworkarchive.com/profile/alex-wilhite]

"I'll tell you later."

The most damaging promise
a hearing family member can make to a Deaf person.

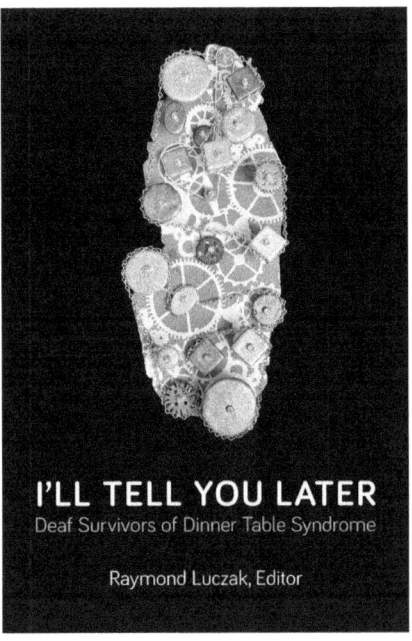

For centuries, Deaf people were expected to sit quietly at the table when their hearing families shared a meal. Some might have asked the person sitting nearby, "What are they saying?" The usual response? "I'll tell you later." When the meal is done, the Deaf person would naturally follow up: "What did they say?" The usual response? "I'm sorry I forgot." Only recently was this transgression given a *name*: Dinner Table Syndrome.

In this anthology, nineteen Deaf and hard of hearing writers share their DTS experiences of anguish and defiance through essays, short stories, and poems, all of which illuminate what it means to be left starving at mealtime.

I'll Tell You Later: Deaf Survivors of Dinner Table Syndrome
Raymond Luczak, Editor

Available from **Handtype Press** and elsewhere
ISBN: 978-1-941960-21-9

www.ingramcontent.com/pod-product-compliance
Lightning Source LLC
Chambersburg PA
CBHW050410030726
47503CB00006B/2124